More Golf Lessons
with MR. X

More Golf Lessons with MR. X

Prentice-Hall, Inc., Englewood Cliffs, N.J.

MORE GOLF LESSONS WITH MR. X

First published in Great Britain by
PELHAM BOOKS LTD

First American Edition published by
Prentice-Hall, Inc., 1972

Copyright © 1971 by Mr. X and GOLF MONTHLY

ISBN 0–13–600684–1

Library of Congress Catalog Card Number: 72–10445

Printed in Great Britain

Contents

ACKNOWLEDGEMENTS

The author's thanks are due to the following for permission to reproduce their copyright photographs in this book:

Frank Gardner: Plates 1, 2, 3, 4, 5, 6, 7, 8, 9, 10, 11, 12, 13, 55, 56, 57. *Press Association:* Plate 14. *G. M. May:* Plates 15, 16, 17, 18, 19, 20, 21, 22, 23, 24. *Golf Monthly:* Plates 25, 26, 27, 28, 29, 30, 31, 32, 33, 34, 35, 36, 37, 38, 39, 40, 41, 42, 43, 44, 45, 46, 47, 48, 49, 50, 51, 52, 53, 54. *Donald Price:* Plates 58, 59, 60, 61, 62, 63, 64, 65. *Chuck Brenkus:* Plates 25–54.

I dedicate this, my second book on golf, to my patient wife Ida.

I must also place it on record how very much I appreciate the valuable help of many golfing friends who have carried out tests for me from time to time.

From the considerable number of letters I have received from golfers in many parts of the world, it is gratifying to know that what I had to say in my first book has been helpful to them.

Unfortunately, it was quite impossible for me to acknowledge so many encouraging and helpful letters. I now take this opportunity of thanking them.

I also thank the critics for their generous acceptance of my first book, in particular: Henry Longhurst of the *Sunday Times*, Peter Dobereiner of the *Observer*, Michael McDonnell of the *Daily Mail*, Ken Bowden of *Golf Digest*, U.S.A., and the British Broadcasting Corporation.

BRENKUS

THE AUTHOR'S OPENING OBSERVATIONS

One of the great difficulties in writing a textbook is to express one's technical knowledge on paper in simple language, with sketches and photographs, that can be easily and correctly understood.

In this, my second book, I have endeavoured to keep to essentials that are best suited to the majority of club golfers, who because of physical defects and limitations have great difficulty in applying orthodox fundamentals.

I have therefore confined my observations to those matters which seem to torment the improver and learner. What I have to say has been well tested and proved helpful to most golfers, in particular to those who appreciate that this book is a TEXTBOOK and has therefore to be read several times from cover to cover, and then as far as possible committed to memory so that its instruction can be applied without having to recall the details.

In particular, I would advise the reader to master the 'K' stance and HEAD PLACEMENT. They are simple to understand and to establish, and when mastered greatly simplify the game.

I hope that when you have read this book, you will have derived a better understanding of the game and its technique.

1. Stance Set-up is so Important

All the top tournament players are as individual in their swing actions as they are in physique. It is possible to recognise a well-known player at a distance by his swing. However, there is a marked similarity in the way in which the most successful of the players line up to the ball and target. There is no reason why club golfers should not be able to benefit from studying the line-up sequence of the Stars.

All of the successful players—both Professional and Amateur—realise how important it is to line up correctly, an essential preamble to a correctly grooved swing and parallel with the target; yet handicap golfers all too often overlook the fact that the swing cannot possibly be right if the stance adjustments necessary to produce a sound 'K' set-up are not made in proper sequence.

Many golfers could benefit if they compared their address position with those of the star performers. Unfortunately golfers who possess action shots taken of the Masters are usually more interested in how they swing than in how they look at address or in its preparation ready for action.

However, there is another way of making comparisons—by taking up an address in front of a mirror. In this way the club golfer should have no difficulty in spotting how he differs from the Stars. Such an examination can be most revealing.

For this purpose, here are featured three highly successful golfers. Bobby Cole of South Africa—Clive Clark—and Michael Bonallack.

From these excellent photographs you can detect a marked similarity in the way they line up to the shot, although they are quite different in physique.

There is a close resemblance in the pattern of their arms and head and clubshaft, also in the positioning of their feet in relation to the ball, and especially in the pattern of their knees which are flexed, forward and inwards—buttressed.

Plate 1. Bobby Cole lining up.   *Plate 2. Michael Bonallack lining up.*

Plate 3. Clive Clark lining up.

Obviously these patterns are not accidental; they have been adopted because such players have discovered from experience that their pedestal must be firm, especially the lower legs from foot to knee.

Other important points to note are that their upper arms are firmly set against their chest and their left arm and clubshaft are almost in a straight line. However, this straight line set-up is most marked with Bonallack; slightly less so with Cole; but more pronounced with Clark. The difference is possibly due to their distribution of weight— the more the weight is right of centre, the more the left arm is angled to the shaft, with the left wrist set in slightly.

Other points worth noting:

COLE has a wider than average stance. His slim build and long legs allow a wide stance.

COLE has the left foot turned out more than the other two.

All have their hands left of centre.

BONALLACK has a stronger left-hand grip—his left hand is a little more on top of the shaft than the other two.

Plate. 4. Another shot of Bobby Cole lining up.

All have their nose several inches behind the position of the ball—almost vertical above the inside edge of their right knee, and all have the ball inside the left heel. COLE holds his head UP the most of the trio; CLARK the lowest head position.

COLE and BONALLACK's Spinal Tilt is more upright than CLARK's.

All have a decided bent knee set-up—and a slight kneeling posture.

COLE appears to have a little more weight on his right foot—about 60/40.

All three photos illustrate fine examples of the 'K' address set-up.

Their posture is firm and proud.

The right foot is square to the line of the shot.

The left foot is slightly angled to the left. This helps to keep the left heel low during the swing, and greatly assists the follow through.

The RIGHT SHIN POST is set to resist the back swing pressures, and the hip joints forward and over their feet.

They are standing on SOFT FEET with the weight slightly towards the heels. Dancing feet disturb the balance.

The left knee is positioned to move obliquely towards centre, but with DRAG from the left foot—Left Toe Peg resistance.

Their heads do not LOLL but are held up at address, with the ears in line with the upper spine.

Note their left thumbs—they curve back sufficiently to enable the shaft to be acutely angled to the left arm without its leverage forcing the left wrist to buckle in and under the shaft. How lucky they are to have such thumbs and good postures.

All great golfers have a straight lower spine, and a pelvis set high in the front, the result of strong abdominal and back muscles.

Most club golfers have kinky spines above the sacrum, and this offsets their posterior which is then difficult to control, but a good golf posture can be quickly established by simple exercises—these exercises are illustrated and described in my first book *Golf Monthly's Lessons With Mr. X.*

2. Placement of the Head at Address

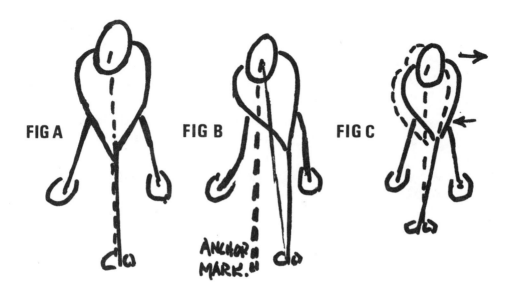

FIG A   FIG B   FIG C

ANCHOR
MARK.

Fig. A

The 'Y' Address (INCORRECT). Player's nose, hands and clubshaft all in line with the ball. Left shoulder too far in advance of ball.

Fig. B

The 'K' Address (CORRECT) Player's nose, several inches to the right of the ball. Hands level with the ball. Eye-line to the ball passes BEHIND the hands.

Fig. C

What NOT to do in the downswing. Player starts in 'K' address position (dotted lines) but, on downswing, responds to subconscious urge to bring his eyes opposite the ball as he is about to strike. Trying to keep the head still can help, but it is not the complete cure.

I regard this single item as one of the essential BASIC FUNDAMENTALS, and yet it is overlooked by thousands of golfers, or they do not obey the rule that insists that we keep the head BEHIND THE BALL WHEN WE HIT IT. Yet in face of this rule, and the teacher's advice to KEEP ONES HEAD STILL, the majority of handicap golfers place their heads central to their feet, instead of RIGHT OF CENTRE where it has to be at impact.

We do not swing a golf club attached to our nose—it is attached to our shoulder extremities, the left shoulder being the CENTRE OF THE SWING, which is about 6 inches away from the nose—so why place our nose opposite the ball, and expect to have it behind the ball at impact. It just can't be done unless we move the head.

Now, why should golfers disobey this simple rule? I will tell you. It is because it is perfectly natural for us humans to BRING OUR EYES opposite an object we are about to strike. It can happen without our knowing, but now you have been made aware of this disastrous fault, you must fight it, and I would suggest that you seek your Professional's assistance in this connection, for it is difficult to see one's actions when swinging a club. Get your Professional to put you into the impact position, with your head back of centre, and your hips well left of centre and into the bow, and then to return you to the address position while he holds your head in the impact position. This will make you aware of the correct head PLACEMENT at address. Go through all the clubs with this drill—putting excepted. Then dispatch a dozen or so balls with each club, HOLDING YOUR HEAD STILL AND DOWN.

I must, however, warn you, when performing as indicated, there is another VILLAIN hiding in the background—MR. POSTURE— usually unrecognised, for it is a physical defect due to neglected abdominal muscles that allow the tummy to protrude and pull the spine inwards at the lower end—what I refer to as the KINKY SPINE. A kinky spine OFFSETS the posterior and prevents our hips from turning and moving laterally in line with the plane of the swing or target line. Instead, offset hips will turn in a scythe-like curve during the swing, and cause the swing to be saucer-like instead of following a true plane. In short, your hip action DESIGNS the plane of the swing without you knowing.

Golfers who are keen to perfect their POSTURE can by simple physical exercises establish a GOLF POSTURE within a few weeks and halve their handicap, even reach scratch. Those who are not prepared to do the exercises as prescribed in my first book, *Golf Monthly's Lessons With Mr. X*, can improve their short game and putting by contracting their abdominal muscles at address, and maintaining this contraction throughout the shot; but for full shots, I fear there is no alternative to exercises—contracted muscles are no substitute for posture by muscular development.

You may have to be convinced that posture is the No. 1 basic fundamental if one is to play golf well, so here is a drill that can produce good results and prove the importance of a straight spine.

Take a 3 or 4 iron. Stand with your left foot in the rough and your right foot in the fairway. Address the edge of the long grass and, with your abdominal muscles contracted, swing into and through the long grass, and note the line cut in it with the clubhead—you will find it is straight and long. Now relax your abdominal muscles and execute a few more swings, and you will see that the blade cuts the grass in a curve to the left. Having convinced yourself that posture is the answer to most of your problems, put a few balls down and dispatch them with your abdominal muscles contracted; the results will thrill you, and shock your opponents. Then go on the putting green and apply the same rule, and watch the putts go down.

Finally, remember to avoid the 'Y' address with your eyes in line with the clubshaft. Cultivate the 'K' address with the left arm and shaft more or less in a straight line and that your eye-line to the ball passes two inches back of your hands.

When the address for all shots—putting excepted—is correct, the 'left shoulder extremity' should be positioned exactly opposite the LOWEST POINT IN THE SWING. For a DRIVE the front edge of the ball—for the irons the middle of the divot hole ahead of the bull.

3. Wrists at the Top

Handicap golfers find it most difficult to get their wrists in correct alignment at the top of the swing.

They either get to the top with the left wrist buckled in and under the shaft, or they go to the opposite extreme and have it bulging upwards.

The former is caused by the player rolling the hands clockwise during the take off, which opens the clubface and angles the left wrist to the shaft. The latter is caused by shutting the clubface excessively with the left hand at the start of the back swing.

The cure for both these disastrous movements is to WIND UP THE MUSCLES OF THE RIGHT FOREARM during the back swing, by hinging the RIGHT WRIST SQUARE TO THE PLANE OF THE SWING when taking off, and not allowing it to turn clockwise. This unnatural and rather uncomfortable action must be mastered, first in the short swings, and subsequently in the full swings.

Study the three photographs accompanying this chapter, and you will see what is really meant by getting the right hand and wrist UNDER the shaft, and the left wrist in line with the left forearm, 'WRINGING THE FLANNEL' at the top.

SNEAD. At the top his left wrist forms a continuous line with the left forearm.

The right wrist and hand have hinged back and are UNDER the shaft, providing a PROP or PLATFORM on which the club rests—this PULLS the left arm STRAIGHT.

The shaft, which would be lying obliquely across the left hand at address, has now altered to a position in which it is parallel to the ROOTS of the fingers, which indicates that the muscles of this hand have yielded a little to the cantileverage of the club—roughly 12 lb.

Note the rake of the shoulders—the right shoulder is well elevated, and the tilt of the spine at address has not altered.

The same analysis applies to SIKES and VICENZO.

Plate 5. Roberto de Vicenzo.

Plate 6. Sam Snead.

Plate 7. Dan Sykes.

These Masters do not tuck their right elbow into their sides like a trussed chicken, but allow it sufficient freedom during the back swing, so that they can reach the top position with their right wrist nicely angled UNDER the shaft.

In the down swing their right elbow DROPS into their side in response to the descent of their right shoulder. The assembly formed by the right shoulder extremity, arms, hands and club starts down in ONE PIECE. It does not alter until the hands are about level with the right hip.

Although it is said that the Masters start the down swing with a downward pull by their left arm, it is my view that they set their action in motion by COMPRESSING their RIGHT SIDE; that is by starting down with their right shoulder extremity directly towards their right foot or knee.

RIGHT SIDE COMPRESSION activates their movements in the following manner.

(*a*) The right shoulder extremity moves vertically down and through towards the target and brings the right elbow into their waist.

(*b*) The hip mass and knees respond by sliding and turning towards the left.

(*c*) The weight moves obliquely from the right foot to the left heel as the result of the thrust from the right foot.

(*d*) The head—a very heavy object—having been positioned RIGHT OF CENTRE at address, keeps down and back and acts as a counter-weight to the hips, moving left of centre and into the BOW.

All great golfers BUTTRESS their right leg from knee to foot—their RIGHT SHIN POST—to resist the wind-up pressures, and assist in bringing the right shoulder, arm and clubhead STRAIGHT UP THE LINE of the shot.

If a golfer lets go with the right shin post during the back swing, his right leg straightens and alters the plane of the swing which sends the ball off line.

4. The Head and the Arms

It is said that a STILL HEAD is the key to a well-executed golf shot.

I doubt this. I have yet to find a Master whose head remains completely still just before, at and after impact. It has to move down during this segment, so as to allow the hips to move into the BOW, but until the hitting segment is reached by the hands it certainly does remain still, but from then onward and until the ball has gone it has to exert DOWNWARD PRESSURE, and action photographs of the Masters clearly confirm this fact.

Why should this be? There is a simple explanation. The heavy head acts as a counterweight to the upward and leftward thrust from the RIGHT FOOT.

If, therefore, the club golfer tries to keep his head still until the ball is dispatched, he will develop SLUGGISH HIP ACTION, and up will come his head and body, especially if his head has been positioned central at address, instead of RIGHT OF CENTRE. Positioning the head central at address is the cause of more bad golf shots than any other fault, so see that your nose is vertically above the inner edge of your right knee for ALL shots—putting excepted.

The ARMS. The arms should be regarded as slings, their upper ends firmly attached to the shoulder extremities, and that they convey propulsion to the clubhead generated by the big muscles of the legs and body. If you can get that concept clear in the mind you are well on the way to better golf.

The arms should not, in themselves, PROVIDE or CREATE propelling power. Countless golfers go wrong in trying to use them in this way.

It may appear, when watching the Masters in action, that they are using their arms to swing the club, but this is an illusion, and

Plate 8. Tony Jacklin. Close analysis of action photographs of Master golfers shows that, in the impact area, the head tends to move BACK slightly, to counter the forward movement of the hip mass. This study of Tony Jacklin, the 1967 Dunlop Master champion, shows his head still well back after impact, and in precisely the same position as it was at impact. It is the bowed position of the body that gives the impression that the head has moved back from its address placement right of centre.

Plate 9. Guy Wolstenholme. Set yourself up to make your arms function as BEAMS to transmit body power, as Guy Wolstenholme has obviously done here.

21

contrary to mechanical laws. For some reason the human eye is attracted to the fast-moving hands and arms, but rarely to the slower-moving HUB.

To work effectively in conveying the central power to the clubhead, the UPPER ARMS should feel BRACED to the shoulder extremities —this will ensure that the swing starts in ONE PIECE. Examine the action photos of the Masters. Their triangle remains intact until the clubshaft is well angled to their left arm, about half-way back.

The HABIT of using one's arms to manipulate things dies hard. From birth we have been educating our hands and arms to grab or slash at things. In golf we have to reverse the process and use our shoulder extremities to swing our arms with power provided by the big muscles of our legs and hips. Somewhat like a weight thrower.

The arms may contribute towards elevating the club towards the end of the back swing, and in the follow through, but momentum of the clubhead provides most of this action. Finally, watch your HEAD PLACEMENT, it is so important, and see that your upper arms are firmly braced to your shoulder extremities immediatley before you take off.

5. The Duty of the Legs

Legs are the PEDESTAL upon which our superstructure is supported They are fundamental to both BALANCE and ACTION.

Doubtless you have noticed when travelling in a bus that the conductor, while making out his log, bends at the knees so as to keep in balance without holding on.

So it is with golf. The player must stand on his LEG MUSCLES and not on his BONES, so he must bend slightly at his knees with a kneeling action—I prefer this to sitting, for the former helps to keep the posterior over the feet, whereas the latter places the posterior more behind the heels.

During the Back Swing: the right knee having been set a little in towards centre—buttress fashion—this leg from the knee to the foot should resist the back-swing pressures—I refer to it as the RIGHT SHIN POST. It must be kept as firm and as still as possible, for it is the only part of our anatomy that can bring us back into the correct hitting position. It is just as important to keep this right knee STILL during the back swing as it is to keep our head still.

Should this RIGHT SHIN POST yield, and the leg straighten, it cannot deliver thrust to the left during the down swing. When straight, all the player can do is to turn his body round on his right hip joint and lose balance, with disastrous results.

Supporting the resistance to the back swing by the Right Shin Post is what I call the LEFT TOE PEG. The duty of the left leg is to enable the hips and shoulders to turn, by its knee yielding inwards towards a point midway between the ball and the right foot. In doing so it must set up DRAG, by preventing the left heel from rising too much in the long shots, and not at all with the shorter clubs. This DRAG

23

Plate 10. At the top of the swing. The player has swung back against a firm, resisting RIGHT SHIN POST, and with left leg resistance also provided by the LEFT TOE PEG anchor.

24

Plate 11, Coming-into impact. The knees are shuttling the hip mass to the left, to keep the clubhead moving in a flat straight line at impact.

must be felt in the muscles up the inside of the left calf. It is this drag that helps the left knee to pull the hips over to the left with a shuttle action similar to the right knee, both knees keeping on the same plane through impact and still bent.

You have heard the expression—KEEP DOWN ON THE SHOT. Many golfers have the impression that this means keeping the head down until after impact, but it is just as important for them to keep the whole of their anatomy down, and this is only possible if the knees stay bent, and in this bent state they have to take most of the outward and downward pull from the clubhead as it moves through the impact area—this pull can be as much as 60 to 80 lb.

You can appreciate that to take this considerable balance disturbing pull with bent legs, it is essential to have very strong leg muscles, especially the thigh muscles. That great Professional golfer, the late Fred Robson of Addington, was heard to say: 'When a golfer's legs weaken, he is on the way out.'

Finally, the reason why the right leg from knee to foot has to be slightly inclined towards centre and treated as a Right Shin Post to resist the wind-up pressures during the back swing, is so that the downward pressure from the head, and especially the RIGHT SHOULDER EXTREMITY, shall force the right knee to SHUTTLE towards centre, and carry with it the hips and help them to DRAG the right shoulder, arms, hands and club—IN ONE PIECE—down and through impact and into the follow through. Some Masters allow this RIGHT SHIN POST to yield a little during the back swing, but when they do so to excess, when out for a long shot, they usually finish up in the woods to the left of the target. My advice, however, to the average golfer is NOT TO LET GO a fraction—keep it firm, and wind up against its resistance, and with THRUST from the right foot—shoot it up the line—during the down swing, but watch not to STRAIGHTEN this leg in so doing—keep up the DOWN pressure until the ball has gone.

6. Swinging the Hook
HINGE and SWING is the THING

One of the best aids to better golf for the handicap golfer is to SWING THE HOOK. Let me explain what this means.

Most handicap golfers have considerable difficulty in hinging the club sufficiently and correctly at the top of the swing, but even if they do, they cannot maintain the acute angle between the left arm and the clubshaft—the Comet's Tail—on the way down; the clubshaft has straightened in line with this arm long before the hands reach the start of the 'hitting' segment which is roughly about the level of the right hip. All the golfer can do is to deliver a weak 'push along' action with the hands and arms.

The 'push along' action creates the following errors:

1. The hands and arms race ahead of the shoulders, hips and knees.
2. The triangle formed by the shoulders—as its base—and the arms—as its two sides—breaks up, and the player's balance is disturbed.
3. The left arm bends at the elbow at, and immediately after, impact.
4. The shot is sliced, hooked or smothered.
5. The speed of the clubhead at impact is greatly reduced, and power is lost.
6. The hands and arms are drawn inwards.
7. Like the skater who flings his arms outwards in order to stop spinning' so the straightening of the shaft to the left arm retards the essential action of the knees hips and shoulders.

27

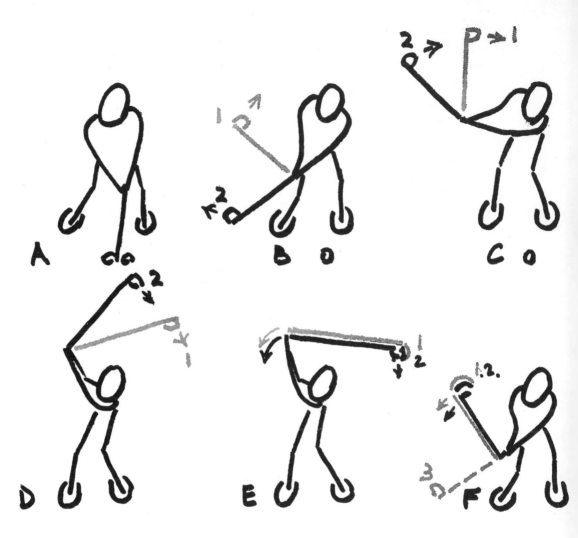

A. The proud 'K' posture for which all golfers should strive at address.

B.1. The early hooked position of the club shaft that I recommend.

B.2. The Masters' method of taking the club back in one piece with the shoulders and arms.

C.1. The hooked position of the shaft when the hands have travelled halfway on the backswing.

C.2. The position of the shaft in the Masters' swing halfway on the backswing.

D.1. The hooked position of the club shaft nearing the top of the swing.

Fig. 2.

D.2. The position of the shaft in the Masters' swing nearing the top of the swing.

E.1. and 2. The top position reached by both methods but by different routes.

F.1 and 2. The late hit angle maintained by both methods.

F.3. The incorrect position that results from handicap golfers trying to imitate the Masters' method of swinging without having the flexible wrists and considerable left thumb yield with which the Masters are endowed.

How then can these errors be avoided? By HOOKING THE CLUB-SHAFT TO THE LEFT ARM early in the back swing but keeping the hands low—they must not lift upwards at the take off.

The HOOK has to be established to at least a right angle by the time the hands have reached waist level, and this hooked assembly is then taken up and over the player's right shoulder extremity.

The important item in establishing the HOOK is to see that the RIGHT WRIST hinges square to the PLANE OF THE SWING; that is to say, the right wrist and hand must not turn the clubface open—this is an unnatural action, so has to be learnt and mastered, and when it is mastered it certainly pays dividends.

When the action has been performed correctly, the wrists at the top of the swing will be positioned as follows: the RIGHT wrist will be under the shaft and the hand will be positioned like a platform supporting the club's weight; the LEFT wrist will be in line with the forearm, and not buckled in and under the shaft. At first this alignment may feel awkward and unnatural, but it is correct and has to be mastered. Watch the action of the RIGHT wrist, for this is the one that matters.

Now for the down swing. Having established the HOOK on the way up to the top, and registered the feel of it, hold on to the hook on the way down. Bring the whole assembly down in ONE PIECE with DRAG. Do not allow the gap between the wrists and right shoulder extremity to open. Have no fear that the clubhead will be left behind at impact, centrifugal force and gravity will see to this; not even a blacksmith's hands and arms are strong enough to stop these forces operating correctly.

When the hands have reached the level of the right hip and the clubhead is still away back and about level with the right shoulder extremity, the forces referred to will start to open the HOOK, and it is at this point that the hands and wrists ADD LEVERAGE TO SWING in the following manner.

The left arm from wrist to shoulder puts up or applies forward resistance, in fact it tries to STOP THE TOP END OF THE CLUBSHAFT AT IMPACT, and at the same time the RIGHT HAND AND WRIST tries to BRUSH PAST the resisting left wrist. It may be thought that such an action would hook the shot when the leverage is applied immediately BEFORE impact, but this will not happen because two things prevent it. One, there is time lag between the brain stimulus and the relative muscular action; and two, there is the terrific force of impact amounting to around half a ton trying to force the clubhead open, so your effort to apply LEVERAGE with the hands and wrists is cancelled out during the period at which the crushed ball is hard against the clubface. If you will examine the photos of the Masters immediately after impact, you will observe the result of this LEVERAGE, their right hand has crawled over the left hand. This crawling over muscular action has in fact been dictated by the brain IN ADVANCE of IMPACT. The Masters may apply the leverage later than the average golfer because their reflexes are faster. With some golfers it may be necessary for them to start the leverage immediately the hands reach the level of the right hip, or even before this.

Most golfers are aware that the swing should start with a One Piece take off—that is, the triangle formed by the arms and shoulders should keep intact until the hands have reached waist level. The same rule applies to the start of the down swing, the hands and arms must on no account RACE AWAY ahead of the hips and shoulders; this is a very common fault, but SWINGING THE HOOK helps one to avoid this error. That which is felt on the way back is much easier to retain on the way down.

Finally, a word of warning. No matter how well one may swing a club, it is absolutely essential to see that the HEAD PLACEMENT is exactly correct at address. By a slight tilt of body to the right, the

HEAD is positioned RIGHT OF CENTRE. The player's nose should be immediately above the inside edge of the RIGHT KNEE. If it is positioned central to the feet, a common error, and unfortunately a natural one, disaster is certain. Get the feel of the correct head placement by standing in front of a mirror—put yourself into the position of the Masters at, or immediately after impact, with the body well into the BOW—then get someone to hold your head still, and bring your body, hips and knees back into the address position. You will then see and feel where your head must be when addressing the ball for ALL shots, even the tiddlers. Putting is the only exception to this rule.

If someone tells you that you have lifted your head, you can be certain that the cause is that YOU HAVE HAD YOUR HEAD CENTRAL TO YOUR FEET at address.

If your head has to be behind your RIGHT KNEE at, and immediately after impact, and you have to keep this heavy object STILL, it follows that it must be in the same position at address, and you must train yourself to look OBLIQUELY at the backside of the ball when addressing it, and NOT straight down at the top of it. It is natural, when about to strike an object you are looking at, to bring the eyes exactly opposite that object—you must fight this villain.

Watch your distance from the ball; for a drive your hands should blot out your left toe-cap; and for an 8 iron they should blot out your left ankle, other clubs in between these points.

In aiming at the target, when placing your feet, and tilting your spine have a peep at your elbows; if you are correctly aligned, your elbows should be SHUT. If they are shut in line to the target then your shoulders will be square to it. It is easier to trust your elbow alignment than to try and square your shoulders; the elbows are below your eyes, your shoulders are NOT in line with your eyes, so it is easy to have them open without knowing it. Should your elbows appear open to the shot-line, you have not tilted your spine enough.

31

7. Giving Width to the Swing

The sketches illustrated in the chapter on 'Swinging the Hook' apply to this chapter.

Most golfers have heard of this phrase, but judging from the way they apply these instructions it would seem that they do not understand what it means, and what effect it has on their action.

Having regard to the mechanical implications, it is my view that, so far as the handicap golfer is concerned, swinging the club back in a wide arc the focal point should be in the movement of the HANDS instead of the CLUBHEAD.

The Masters undoubtedly favour the latter and cock their wrists at the top of the swing—their wrists are better trained to yield without bouncing the clubhead away from their axis—but I think the handicap golfer would do better by using the former method and HINGE and SWING the club, keeping the hands low during the first quarter of the back swing, in other words getting width with the HANDS, and hinging the right wrist squarely back immediately after the take off.

My reason for advocating the HINGE and SWING method has many advantages for the handicap golfer, the most important of which is that by hinging the club to the left arm early it considerably reduces the cantileverage strain on the arms for it brings the clubhead rapidly nearer the players axis, and is not so likely to disturb balance and cause sway.

Another important advantage is that when the clubshaft is angled early to the left arm—that is HOOKED to it—it is much easier to retain the HOOK on the way down, which is a most important feature in a correct swing for it adds both speed and power to the clubhead coming in for impact. That which is felt on the way back is much easier to retain on the way down—SWINGING THE HOOK as it were.

The important point when using the HINGE and SWING method is that when the right wrist starts to hinge back square to the plane of the swing, the hands must not LIFT but keep LOW, for it is their lowness of movement that makes the shoulder extremities perform their somewhat steep spiral sweeps as they turn. If they lift, the shoulder extremities will turn in a shallow sweep and produce a flat swing. Keeping the upper arms braced to the chest ensures that the triangle formed by the shoulders and arms is maintained and the back swing will take off in ONE PIECE. On no account should the upper arms feel sloppy or relaxed at the shoulder joints. It is essential that the big muscles provide the motive power—SWING FROM THE SHOULDER EXTREMITIES is the right attitude.

By the time the hands have completed the first half of the back swing, the player should feel that the clubshaft is HOOKED TO THE LEFT ARM, and that this HOOK is being carried up to the TOP and then DOWN again, that the clubhead is away back, and is being DRAGGED down like a Comet's Tail. No attempt must be made to undo the HOOK—centrifugal force and gravity will do this most efficiently without any help from the hands and wrists, and with tremendous speed; there is an outward and downward pull from the clubhead of about 60 lb. at impact which straightens the clubshaft to the player's left arm automatically.

Here are some simple exercises for the development of the Hinge and Swing method.

1. Without any swinging action, learn to hinge the RIGHT WRIST back square to the plane of the swing as near a right angle as possible to the left arm. When doing this exercise, do not move the hands away from the address position. This is purely a wrist exercise, the purpose of which is to train the muscles of the wrists and forearms to hinge square to the plane of the swing—there must be no turning of the wrists in either direction.

33

Plate 12

Plates 12 and 13. Clive Clark and Bernard Gallacher. Giving width to the swing. Keep the hands low going back during the first quarter of the backswing. This study of Clive Clark shows it being done. Handicap players frequently 'lift' the hands too quickly. What they should do is to keep the hands low, starting back but elevate the clubhead sooner than the Masters do by hingeing the right wrist square to the plane of the swing, as illustrated in the photo of Bernard Gallacher.

Plate 13

2. Having done the wrist action a dozen times, then firm the upper arms to the chest, and move the hands back LOW, at the same time hinging the club back on the right wrist and carry on until the shaft is well HOOKED to the left arm. Then proceed to hook the club over the right shoulder extremity.

3. At the top of the swing, HALT, and have a look at the alignment of your hands and wrists, also the clubface.

(a) Your right wrist and hand should be UNDER or almost under the shaft. The clubface should be angled at about 45 degrees to the sky, and the left wrist should be almost in line with the forearm. On no account should the left wrist be buckled in and under the shaft; if it is, then you have turned your wrists clockwise and opened the clubface on taking off. Watch that right wrist on taking off, for this is the one that matters.

Now, the STARTING DOWN exercise.

(b) As so few golfers have a well-developed left arm, it is difficult for them to control the club with it as the Masters do. Fortunately there is an alternative method which is most effective, and in my view more suitable for the handicap golfer.

When the hands and club have reached the top, or a fraction before top, the RIGHT SHOUDLER EXTREMITY is made to take charge and sweep straight downwards towards the right foot or right knee and then carried past the ball and on towards the target.

The downward sweep of the right shoulder exerts pressure on the right knee and sends it with the hips leftward. Shoulder rotation follows naturally as the result of the twisted muscles of the back unwinding, and as they unwind the left hip turns out of the way of the oncoming right hip, shoulder and club as they come STRAIGHT UP THE LINE. This sequence of actions sends the hips into the BOW, and keeps the head back and down.

When practising this RIGHT SIDE COMPRESSION control, make sure that at address your spine is sufficiently tilted to the right in order that your head is positioned right of centre, and your nose is vertically above the inner side of the right knee, and that it stays there until after impact.

Finally, endeavour to keep your left arm as straight as possible after the ball is dispatched.

With the HINGE and SWING METHOD, you should try swinging the club first with the left arm in control, and then with the right in control, and note which gives you the best results.

It is important, however, when swinging with the right arm that the right wrist and hand does not roll the clubface open at the take off by turning clockwise. This can happen if your mind is on keeping your right elbow stuck into your waist; no great golfer does this going back, only when he is coming down, and then it does so in response to the descent of the right shoulder extremity, and the inertia pull from the club.

I have been asked many times whether the Masters use their right hand wrist and arm with restraint; I would say that some do and some don't, but one thing is certain: when their hands have reached about right hip level, all of them use all the power they can produce with the right shoulder extremity, right arm and hand to propel the clubhead coming in for impact; that is for the full shots, with the shorter shots to a less degree.

This does not mean that the left arm is a sloppy passenger. Its duty is to maintain the radius from shoulder to clubhead, or in other words to KEEP STRAIGHT at, and as long as it is possible after, impact. Examine the pictures of the Masters a quarter through after impact; their left arm is fully extended; then watch the handicap golfers on the course and note how their left arm has buckled immediately the ball is hit. These are the arm swingers, the masters are the shoulder extremity swingers from address until in the down swing their hands have reached the level of their right hip, and then WHAM! with their RIGHT HAND AND ARM through impact and on TOWARDS THE TARGET.

Many handicap golfers would, I am sure, play better golf if they controlled the swing with their RIGHT HAND WRIST AND ARM—PROVIDED they concentrated upon HINGING THE RIGHT WRIST BACK SQUARE TO THE PLANE OF THE SWING at take off, and during the first half of the back swing.

8. Swinging into the Bow

Plate 14.

In this excellent photo we have a classic example of SWINGING INTO THE BOW.

The subject is Bernard Gallacher, the brilliant young Scot.

The features that combine to create the bow-like action are evident from a finish of the swing study—leftward thrust from the right foot has sent the hips and knees through and into the bow, while the head has held back and down. The forward momentum of the action has carried Gallacher over on to the OUTER edge of his left heel.

As I believe it is easier to learn golf from IMAGE than by FEEL, here is one important picture to work on when on the practice ground.

Prior to playing a shot, try and visualise yourself arriving in this position—the blow-like poise of the Master immediately after dispatching the ball.

Provided you do not go at it too hard, you should have no difficulty in producing this profoundly important IMAGE when actually swinging the club. You can check on whether or not you are achieving it with the aid of a mirror, or better still under the eye of a qualified teacher. Ten minutes of this practice is worth hours of aimlessly hitting balls.

Now for the address POSTURE that makes the action possible.

In my first book I named the golf posture address as the 'K' address, because it resembled a capital K in reverse, and the illustration described had lines drawn on the photo to show how the Masters' stance fitted in to the letter K.

Watch your head placement at address, as it governs the correct position of the left shoulder extremity relative to the lowest point in the swing. so at address it must be stationed in the same place as it should be immediately before, at and after impact.

This placement of the head is NOT NATURAL; the natural position is central to the feet, which is wrong, so you have to learn where the head has to be stationed correctly if the command to 'keep it still' is worth obeying, and the best place to do the drill is in front of a mirror, or seek the help of your Professional.

When you look at a good golfer in action, immediately before, at and after impact, you may get the impression that his head has fallen back and down, but in actual fact it has moved very little, possibly not at all; the illusion is caused by the considerable leftward curve of his body, what I call the ARCHER's BOW. When the bow is fully bent, the extremities of the bow come nearer together, so it follows that the golfer's head must drop slightly at impact, but not move laterally, as this would shift the centre of his swing.

I believe it is money well spent for golfers to go to their Professional. Ask him to push them into a good impact position, with the hips bowed well left of centre, and the head right of centre, and immediately above a point on the ground midway between centre and the inner edge of the sole of the right shoe; then to hold the head still, and get you to bring the body and legs back to the correct position—that is the 'K' set-up. The pupil should then take stock of himself and feel the correct address position of the head, in particular how the eyes are looking obliquely at the BACK of the ball. When you can move immediately into the correct 'K' address position, get on with hitting a few balls under the watchful eye of your tutor—YOU will be pleased with the results, and so will your TEACHER. He is just as anxious to improve your game as you are. A pupil that makes progress is the Professional's best advocate.

I have gone to some length in telling you about this profoundly important HEAD PLACEMENT; now I shall tell you why it must be stationed RIGHT of CENTRE at address and at impact. It is because the HEAVY HEAD has to act as a COUNTER-WEIGHT to the thrust from the right foot and divert its force obliquely towards the left shoulder and hip.

If you obey your natural instinct, and position the head central to the feet at address, it will NOT operate as a counter-weight but will be driven up and along towards the target. Doubtless you have seen many golfers chasing the clubhead with their head and right shoulder during impact. This ugly action is called 'HEAD UP' by those who do not know that the cause is BAD HEAD PLACEMENT at address.

I have come across a few good players who position their heads central to their feet and still manage to get the ball away nicely, but they moved their head and shoulders about 4 inches to the right immediately on starting the back swing and then kept their heads still. I should mention that all of these golfers had started playing golf at a very early age, and were quite unaware that they played with this unorthodox method. I have explained this method in chapter 21 should you wish to test it.

9. Don't Let Your Head Loll at Address

DON'T LOLL
the right and wrong address positions

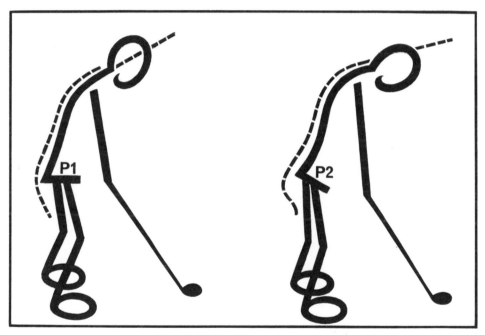

RIGHT—*Pelvis (P1) UP.*   WRONG—*Pelvis (P2) TILTED.*

Fig. 3.

As a rule, golfers do not realise how devastating an effect a 'lolling head' can have on their performance.

Good golfers do not let their heads drop on to their chests.

The head is a very heavy part of the human body, so if it is allowed to drop downwards and forwards, the posterior acting as a compensating weight will stick out to the rear.

This bad set-up results in loss of balance during the swing, and is frequently the cause of HEAD UP.

The two sketches show the good and bad set-up.

Sketch No. 1 shows the correct set-up. Points to note are.

The player's ears are in line with the upper spine. Address a ball and get someone to check your alignment, and if necessary adjust it—then register the feel of the erect head.

The buttocks do not stick out.

The pelvis basin is almost parallel with the ground, and the hip joints are over the feet and not behind them; the lower spine is almost straight.

The player with this desirable set-up should be conscious of the following feel

The posture feels PROUD.

The CROWN of the head feels high and the chin feels IN.

The torso feels EXTENDED without being rigid.

Sketch No. 2 shows the incorrect set-up:

The back of the head is in line with the upper spine. It feels down, and the chin is out.

The head and shoulders will tend to spin round at impact and move in the direction of the target, and the posterior will remain behind, or even move away from the target instead of into the BOW. No doubt you have seen this dreadful action many times on the course.

To rectify this fault, here is a simple exercise that will pay dividends.

Lie on the floor face downwards, and raise and lower the head and shoulders a few inches several times daily. Within a month you will find that you will hold your head erect when addressing the ball, and your golf will improve. Check yourself in a mirror now and then to see if your head stations itself correctly without being forced to do so.

10. Locking the Gap
A Vital NEW Concept of the Golf Swing

A great deal has been written about the importance of the ONE PIECE TAKE AWAY in starting the back swing, but little has been said about the importance of making a ONE PIECE start of the down swing.

For years golfers have been told NOT TO HIT FROM THE TOP, yet few seem to have been able to obey this important advice, even though it is quite clear that hitting from the top is one of the actions that can destory a golf swing. Unfortunately, it is natural to use the arms and hands to hit at objects, the habit starts from the moment we are born. So thousands of handicap golfers continue to lash at the ball from the top of the swing with their hands and arms, when in fact it is the big muscles of our legs and body that provide the motive power.

It would seem that the ordinary golfer has failed to eradicate this fault because he does not have a clear picture of the correct action he should try and achieve. It is one thing to be told 'Do not hit from the top'; quite another to discover the POSITIVE action that will eliminate the fault.

The positive action can be acquired, for it is evident in the swings of every good golfer, so let us see how it can be mastered.

In a good swing, the gap separating the wrists from the right shoulder extremity at the top of the swing remains unchanged during the early stage of the down swing. If, however, it does widen, the player will instantly hit from the top with his hands and arms.

The width of this GAP varies a little—about 12 inches for the handicap golfer, and about 10 inches for the Master.

44

1. *Upper arms locked to shoulders.*

2. *Halfway on the backswing.*

3. *Top of swing—Gap-lock established.*

4. *Downswing—Gap-lock maintained.*

5. *Gap-lock now beginning to open.*

6. *Upper arms locked to shoulders.*

Fig. 4.

45

Whatever the width of the gap, it must be maintained until the hands descend to about waist level.

It is in my view one of the most important things in golf, and the golfer should endeavour to master the art of LOCKING THE GAP.

There are several ways of tackling the art, but I think the simple way is to imagine when the top of the swing is reached that the wrists are STRAPPED to the right shoulder extremity, and remain so until the hands have descended to about waist level during the down swing.

THE DRILL. When you have reached the top of the back swing, and locked the gap, you then DRIVE the right shoulder extremity VERTICALLY DOWNWARDS TOWARDS THE RIGHT FOOT—not the ball— dragging the hands and club along with it in ONE PIECE; they must remain PASSIVE and RELAXED.

It is frequently said that the down swing should be started by the left arm pulling the club down, or by shifting the hips over to the left, but I am convinced that such actions are the result of the downward sweep of the right shoulder extremity. The Master may feel that his left arm is in control, but I do not think that it provides the power but that it merely conveys it.

What the right shoulder does is to produce an opposite action in the lefts houlder, causing it to move upwards and round in a spiral sweep—it is this action of the left shoulder that applies DRAG to the left arm, which the expert golfer feels, but which I am convinced results from RIGHT SIDE COMPRESSION.

When you have mastered this POSITIVE action by indoor practice, go out on the practice ground or driving range with a 6 or 7 iron and dispatch a few balls. Swing smoothly to the tempo of the phrase One AND Two; do not hurry the AND segment, the slower you execute the AND the easier it is to establish the GAP LOCKED. It is a deliberate action.

Another very good exercise that gives you the LOCKED feeling, is, with your back to a wall, swing a club to the top, and get someone to attach the clubhead to a nail in the wall with string or very strong elastic. Then pull down with your right shoulder extremity as if trying to dislodge the clubhead from its anchorage. You will at once notice how the pressures that develop, force the hips and knees over towards the target and rotates the left hip out of the way. You will be made to realise what really activates the hips and knees during the down swing. When actually playing shots the inertia drag from the clubhead acts somewhat like the wall anchor in the exercise prescribed.

I must mention that when the clubhead is put into reverse at the top of the swing, this inertia which results from the club's canti-leverage and momentum can amount to as much as 12 lb. according to the speed of the sweep of the right shoulder extremity and the hips. The great golfers move their knees, hips and shoulder extremi-ties very fast during the down swing so as to use the club's inertia to hold the club well angled to the left arm—the COMET's TAIL.

With some golfers the Gap Lock gives them the feeling that their hands remain behind as the right shoulder extremity moves down-wards. Some register the feeling that the hands move nearer the right shoulder extremity an instant before the clubhead is reversed. Others feel that it is the shoulders that are swinging the clubhead. In all three, the shoulder sweep feels very solid, with the upper arms TRUSSED to them.

You have heard the saying—WAIT FOR IT—at the top. Let the wait for it coincide with LOCKING the GAP.

11. An Open Stance May Suit You Better

So many handicap golfers find it difficult to bring their right side through at impact because their left hip does not get out of the way, with the result that the hips become locked, and when this happens the shoulders spin round and force the head to lift and chase the clubhead.

Much of this trouble arises from a kinky spinal posture which prevents the hip mass moving in line with the plane of the swing—the hips tend to move in a curve or scything action immediately the swing starts. To check this undesirable hip movement it is advisable to try out an OPEN STANCE, as this tends to prevent the right hip slewing round behind the left foot during the back swing, and then returning in a similar curve during the down swing which will cause the clubhead to return to the ball from OUT to IN and slice the shot.

The right way to establish a correct open stance is to take up a square stance first, and then open it by drawing the left foot straight back a little from the ball and target line, at the same time turning the left toe slightly to the left.

By following this drill, you ensure that the ball's position is inside the left heel, and the radius from the left shoulder to the ball is not disturbed. If you try to go straight into the open stance without taking up the square stance first, you are likely to lay your shoulders open as well as your hips and the ball will be positioned opposite your left toe.

In finalising the stance, be sure to tilt the spine and head so as to bring the head right of centre. The nose should be vertically above the INSIDE OF THE RIGHT KNEE, and there it remans throughout the swing. On no account must the head be central, the eyes for ALL golf shots must be trained to look OBLIQUELY at the back of the ball. This may seem a small matter, but it is of profound importance for the head placement, and the oblique view of the ball ensures that the head keeps back and down during impact; the wrong placement of the head, and the wrong look at the ball, is certain to ruin the shot, as the head will lift and the left shoulder turn away during impact.

The heavy head is the counter-weight to our hip mass, so if it is not positioned right of centre at address, the hips will not move into the bow well left of centre.

When watching the Masters in action, the majority of golfers are under the impression that they move their heads considerably to the right as well as down as they come in for impact. They are mislead because of the considerable curve in their bodies as they move into the bow, but in fact their heads move very little from the address position, for they set the head right of centre to start with; this is rarely noticed, but if you will take a photo of them at address and at impact, and draw a perpendicular line from the inside of their right foot on both photos, you will see that their heads hardly move a fraction. This is why they tell their pupils to keep their heads still during the swing. The problem with the pupils is that IT IS NATURAL for them to place their heads CENTRAL and their eyes opposite the ball. If pupils were made to take up the Master's impact position, and with their heads held in this position by the teacher made to return their bodies, hips and legs to the address position, they would realise where their heads should be in relation to the right knee when addressing the ball. Their first reaction to this simple exercise is usually one of amazement, but one of excitement when they execute shots from this set-up.

12. If only I Could Putt

How often we hear this remark made by golfers.

Nothing can be more frustrating than to reach the green in the correct number of strokes and then to take three putts.

Many of my golfing associates have pressed me to include a chapter on putting in this book.

The method I am going to describe has been well tested and found most effective and reliable.

What then goes wrong, when putting goes off? Why should it happen one day and not the next? Is it mental or physical? The answer is that it is usually both.

THE MENTAL SIDE

What should engage our thoughts before and during the stroke?

We have to consider the line, the strength, and how we look at the ball. Each must be considered in their proper sequence and without haste if what we are looking at is to be clearly photographed in the mind.

When considering the line, it should be viewed from behind the ball for level or up hill putts, and from behind the hole for down hill putts. Look up the line from its lowest end.

When considering strength, it should be gauged from the side of the putt, about midway between the ball and hole, care being taken to note the slant of the grass, especially near the hole.

Having made mental records of these two essentials, forget them, and pay attention to seeing the markings on the ball, after having arranged the stance.

As regards stance, I favour the OBLIQUE stance. Here it is.

Place a club on the ground, touching the back of the ball at one end, and at right angles to the line of the putt and towards the feet.

Place the putter blade against the shaft on the ground behind the ball.

Then place the right toe and left heel against the shaft, on the ground the left foot left of the shaft and the right foot right of the shaft, with both feet turned towards the left to a point 6 inches ahead of the ball; the feet should now be in a square turned obliquely to the line of the putt. The blade, right toe and left heel should now be in a straight line exactly at right angles to the line of the putt.

You will now be ready to execute the putt, and it is at this point that the eyes must see the ball very clearly, for if they don't, disturbing thoughts will well up, such as line and strength, and cause the eyes to turn away from the ball before the blade strikes it.

THE PHYSICAL SIDE

We have now to consider the mechanics of the putting action.

The players nose is over the ball, and the arms and clubshaft form a capital 'Y'. The left arm is sufficiently bent at the elbow to ensure that the shoulder extremities are level, or nearly so. They should not be tilted.

Because the putter blade is set at an angle to its shaft, it follows that when taking off the blade has no longer the support of the ground, so gravity tries to bring it in towards the player's feet if the muscles of the arms, wrists and hands are not trained to resist the pull. It is for this reason that the Masters practice putting a great deal. Few club golfers can afford to spend so much time in this department, so for this reason I recommend a light putter, and a TWO FISTED GRIP—the right hand below the left, or the left hand below the right; the latter is well worth trying, although it may feel a bit awkward at first, and it has many advantages.

If you have a fairly heavy putter blade, attach a piece of sheet lead 1 inch wide and about 4 inches long round the top of the shaft with insulating tape; this will make the blade feel lighter when swinging it.

51

When addressing the ball with the blade, place the SOCKET against the ball if a blade putter, and the shaft if a centre shaft putter. Grip softly, and execute the putt.

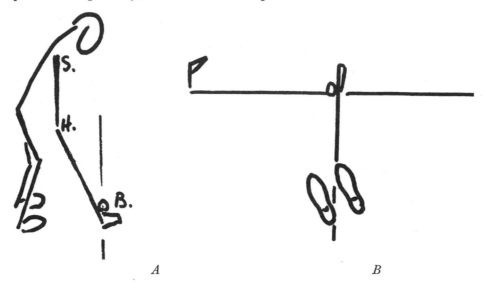

A *B*

Sketch A. THE SOCKET ADDRESS. KNEEL don't SIT. Eyes over the ball. Keep your buttocks and abdomen in. Keep your PEDESTAL STILL. No weight movement.

Sketch B. THE OBLIQUE STANCE. Ball against socket of blade. Left heel and right toe in line with blade. Feet angled slightly left and parallel to one another.

Fig. 5.

Provided you make no attempt to steer the blade, you will find that the centre of the blade will return to the ball because of gravity. To convince yourself that this is so, ask a friend to watch from your right-hand side. Just swing.

Regarding the placement of the hands on the putter, the shaft should lie along the valley of the left hand from the root of the middle finger to the centre of the wrist with the tips of the fingers visible. The right hand should be attached to the shaft so that the right wrist is EXACTLY at RIGHT ANGLES to the line of the putt, so that the wrist will hinge square to the plane of the swing.

Immediately prior to taking off, raise the wrists slightly, as this final adjustment prevents the wrists from rolling the clubface open during the back swing and rolling it shut at impact.

Kneel—don't sit. The former brings your seat more over your feet, instead of behind your heels.

Raise the front of your pelvis by contracting your abdominal muscles, and keep it up throughout the stroke.

Time the action to the One AND Two phrase, and don't hurry the AND. Many of the greatest putters actually HALT the back swing before allowing the blade to return to the ball. They do this by firming the right wrist as the blade leaves the ball, and then LOCK it during the down swing.

13. Which is Your Master Eye?

It is important that golfers should discover which eye is their master eye, and the way to find whether it is the left or right eye is as follows:

With either arm fully extended, point the index finger at some object in the distance with BOTH eyes open.

Now shut your left eye and note whether your finger is still pointing at the object.

Open both eyes, and this time shut your right eye, and note if your finger is pointing at the object. If it is not, but appears to be pointing right of the object, then your RIGHT EYE IS THE MASTER EYE.

It is important when swinging a club that your master eye does not lose sight of the ball's image, especially at the top of the swing.

To make quite sure that it does not lose sight of the ball, take the club to the top of the swing, and shut the left eye.

If the bridge of your nose blots out the ball, then get back to the address position, shut your left eye and swing back until your nose starts to blot out the ball, and note how far back you have swung the club. This is as far as you should swing your club. If you go beyond this point your left eye will take charge and, like your pointing finger, the ball image will appear to have moved and the aim will have altered to a position right of its actual position.

I am inclined to think that this apparent SHIFT OF THE OBJECT tends to make the clubhead strike the ground behind the ball. Golfers can test this out by addressing the ball with, say, a 5 iron, and before taking off shut their left eye and execute the shot and see what happens. I think they will find that the ball is taken cleanly and followed by a good divot. Be careful not to open the left eye during the action.

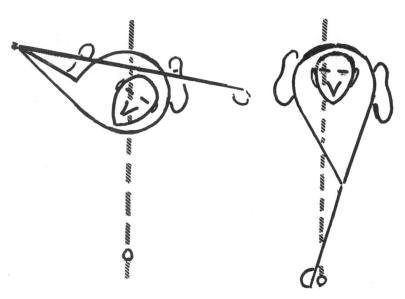

Right—At address this golfer can see the ball with both eyes

Left—At the top of the swing this golfer cannot see the ball with his right eye. The bridge of his nose intervenes.

Fig. 6.

14. Hitting the Ground Behind the Ball

One of the most demoralising and frustrating things that so often happens—particularly when playing the tiddlers around the green—is hitting the ground behind the ball, usually attributed to HEAD UP.

There are several causes, and I will endeavour to explain the causes, and the cures.

CAUSE

Not looking at the ball long enough to read its details before taking off. This causes the player to look up or look round at the target before striking the ball.

Sitting down too much when addressing the ball.

CURE

When playing shots near the green the mind usually pays too much attention to the line and the strength of the shot than to the ball. READ THE BALL PROPERLY and register the line and strength of the shot before taking up the stance.

Once the stance is completed, DON'T look again at the target or disturbing thoughts will engage your mind—trust your feet line. Position your head right of centre, and SEE the divot mark after the ball has gone.

KNEEL—don't SIT. Kneeling keeps your centre of gravity over your feet. Sitting places it behind your heels.

56

Shoulders open at address. Head too central to feet.

See that your elbows are SHUT slightly to the shot line. This ensures that your shoulders are square to the target. See also that your UPPER arms are firmly BRACED to the shoulder extremities.

Forgetting to brace the right knee inwards so as to resist the back swing pressures.

Establish a very firm right leg from knee to foot—buttressed—I call this set the RIGHT SHIN POST. It must resist the back swing, and act like a recoil spring by sending the knees and hips towards the target as the down swing starts. It is the down swing trigger.

Swinging the clubhead much too fast to a One Two tempo. Turning the hands clockwise and opening the blade at the take off.

Swing the clubhead to a One AND Two tempo, and don't hurry the AND.

See that the right wrist hinges back squarely to the plane of the swing, this winds up the right forearm muscles during the back swing. This wrist action is sometimes called CUDDLING THE CLUBHEAD.

Placing the weight on to the soles of the feet.

Place the weight more towards the heels than the soles and kneel —don't sit when the weight is so positioned.

57

An insufficient hinging of the wrists as the club is taken back and reversed.

HINGE AND SWING instead of Swing and Cock the wrists. Hinge the club back early in the back swing. The hand leverage to produce this should hinge the right wrist back squarely to the plane of the swing, so that it is UNDER the shaft at the top and acts as a platform on which the club rests for full swings, and on top for short swings.

Sloppy abdominal muscles and in consequence a KINKY spine. Such a posture plays havoc with the swing.

If your corset muscles have weakened by neglect and soft living, BRACE them by CONTRACTING the ABDOMINAL MUSCLES. This takes the kink out of the lower spine and brings the HIP JOINTS MORE OVER THE FEET at address—but see that you maintain this inward set of the abdomen.

15. Mental Attitudes and Conceptions

There are many tuitional phrases in common use which, no matter how well intentioned they are, can be misleading and make the game more difficult.

NO

Hit the Ball

This tends to encourage a fast snatchy action performed mainly by the arms swiping at the ball from the top of the swing.

Swing Slowly

This tends to make the player LIFT the club up with the arms, and stiffens the forearm muscles. Clubhead inertia, so important at the start of the down swing in order to hold the wrists cocked is lost, and the 'late hit angle' between the left arm and shaft opens far too soon.

YES

Sweep the Ball Away

This encourages a smooth flowing action. It prevents violence, and generates a PROLONGED FORWARD BLOW applied mainly by the RIGHT HAND during impact. The RIGHT HAND BRUSHING OVER a RESISTING LEFT HAND AND ARM. A kind of hand leverage added to swing.

Swing Smoothly

This prevents violence and keeps the wrists relaxed so that they can yield to the pull from the clubhead and establish the late hit angle as well as retain it until the hands have come down to hip level. It is the retention of the late hit angle that sends the clubhead through the ball at great speed, and stimulates snappy wrist action.

Keep Your Eye on the Ball
It is possible for the eyes to see the ball as a white blob with the eyes out of focus.

Slide the Hips Left when Starting the Down Swing
This usually generates a DUNCH-ING ACTION with the shoulders to the left, and an excessive movement of weight on to the left leg. This prevents the right hip and side coming through and stops them turning. When this happens, the shoulders spin round at impact and the ball is sliced.

Take the Clubhead Back in a Wide Arc
This lengthy extension of the left arm and shaft so increases cantileverage pull from the clubhead that it tends to unbalance the player and make him sway to the right. It may be all right for the Masters but dangerous for the average golfer.

See the Ball's Marking Clearly
It is only when the eyes see the details on the ball's surface clearly, does the mind free itself from other disturbing thoughts.

Drive the Right Shoulder Down Towards the Right Foot
This downward compression from the right shoulder sends the right knee and hips to the left and keeps the head down and back, and leaves room for the right shoulder to come straight up the line towards the target—down and through.

Get Width by Keeping the Hands Low
This enables the player to HINGE AND SWING by cocking the right wrist square to the plane of the swing immediately the swing starts.

This considerably reduces the cantileverage pull from the clubhead, and helps to establish the late hit angle between the left arm and the clubshaft on the way up, and maintains it on the way down. Swing OVER and not ROUND oneself.

16. On the Practice Ground

YOUR GRIP

Don't squeeze the blood out of your hands by holding too tightly.

Muscles need blood. Bloodless hands are lifeless hands.

See how relaxed you can hold the club with the hands and swing the club without letting go. Instinctive contraction of the fingers at impact can add yards to your shot.

If you have a stiffish left thumb, push it down the shaft as a final pre-swing adjustment, so as to square the shaft to the roots of the fingers; this helps you to maintain the acute angle between the shaft and the left arm coming down; the orthodox oblique grip tends to open this important angle too soon.

Don't play golf with shiny leather grips; they make you grip too tightly, and stiffen your wrists, Renew them with rubber grips if you are not prepared to look after leather grips and dress them regularly.

Soak your hands in hot water before you practice or play a round. It makes them sensitive to movement. The Masters can use a firm grip on the club, and still keep their wrists flexible—you can't.

YOUR POSTURE

Don't LOLL over the ball at address—stand proudly to the 'K' set-up.

Feel the back of your neck against your collar, and see that YOUR HEAD IS POSITIONED RIGHT OF CENTRE, and not central to your feet. This is a MUST for ALL shots—putting excepted.

The more your head flops down and forward, the more your posterior will poke out to the rear and swing around like a sack of potatoes. Contract your abdominal muscles at address and keep them braced throughout the swing.

The straighter you have the spine at its lower end, with the hip joints forward and over your feet, the easier it is to play golf, especially the short game. A figure 'S' or 'C' spine makes golf very difficult.

Remember that it is natural to bring the eyes opposite the object you are about to strike. It can happen at address, and also immediately before impact—both lead to disaster and cause head up and leftward sway. The head must be positioned RIGHT OF CENTRE and kept there throughout the swing. This is easier said than done, but you have to master it and get used to looking obliquely at the backside of the ball.

STANCE

The golf stance is a FLAT-FOOTED one. You don't have to leap about when playing a golf shot—the ball is stationary.

With the left toe slightly turned out, and the right toe in line with it and the target and the foot square to the target is a reliable stance, as it slightly shuts the heels and makes it easier to pivot.

Kneel, don't sit. The former brings the hip mass more over your feet, whereas the latter tends to position it behind your heels.

If your back muscles are stiff, narrow your stance to the width of your shoulders for the long shots, and about the width of your head for the tiddlers.

Wear good fitting shoes, preferably with low heels. Normal heels are inclined to push you forward and off balance during impact.

When finalising your stance, make a habit of screwing the sole of your right shoe well into the ground. A slight sinkage of this foot during the swing can alter your radius to the ball, and can cause you to take ground behind the ball.

Wear a clean pair of socks each time you play Nothing tires the feet more than damp socks that have worn thin.

YOUR HEAD

Instead of trying to keep your head still, make it your intention to KEEP IT DOWN AND BACK, and see that it is positioned RIGHT OF CENTRE throughout the swing from address to the follow through.

When the head is correctly poised at address, the line of the upper spine should pass through the ears, and not past the back of the head—a common failing with many golfers.

THE ARMS

Use your arms to TRANSMIT propelling power and not to PRODUCE it. The knees, hips and shoulders combine to generate power, and transmit it through the arms to the clubhead. When this is done correctly, the arms DRAG the club along instead of PUSHING it along.

Make it a habit of keeping the upper arms firmly attached to the shoulder extremities. Because of the ever-present changing pull of the club upon the arms, there is a tendency for it to splay the elbows and wrists apart, so destroying the triangular formation created by the shoulders and arms. It is essential that this assembly is maintained during the back swing until the hands have reached waist level, and again immediately before, at and after impact. After impact the maximum effort should be made to keep the left arm extended as long as possible.

The left arm during impact should in fact form part of the LEFT SIDE RESISTANCE to the FORWARD BRUSHING, driving pressure from the right hand and arm. HIT AND STOP with the left arm, as recommended by the Maestro Henry Cotton, is excellent advice—mechanical laws support this. Mechanically, the top of the shaft should stop for an instant during impact. The feeling in this arm should be that it has closed into the chest with a reverse action. I have explained in another part of this book the HAND LEVERAGE added to SWING that accompanies this left arm resistance.

LINING UP FOR THE SHOT
—THE PROFESSIONALS' METHOD

When placing the clubhead behind the ball at address, regard it as the ANCHOR around which you will build up your stance and posture and do not lift the clubhead off the ground until the drill is completed.

Position the hands opposite the lowest point in the swing—OPPOSITE the ball for a drive, and opposite the centre of the divot for the irons, and keep them there until the stance is completed.

Now direct your eyes towards the target, and move yourself into the position that brings your ELBOWS slightly shut to the line of the shot; this should bring your shoulders in line with the target. This completes the drill.

Be careful, however, that your spine as been tilted a little to the right so as to bring your head RIGHT OF CENTRE, and your eyes are looking at the backside of the ball.

If your eyes notice the shaft alignment, you may get the impression that it is angled to the right of the target—an illusion. Do not be tempted to bring it in line with them so that you are looking down the shaft. When angled to the right of the target, it is in fact square to the target, and in line with the left shoulder extremity which is the centre of the swing from address to impact. Your eyes are several inches right of your left shoulder, hence the illusion.

LINING UP FOR THE SHOT—THE MECHANICAL WAY

Place the clubhead on the ground 6 or 7 inches to the right of the lowest point in the swing—for a drive 5 to 6 inches to the right of the ball—for an 8 iron, 5 or 6 inches to the right of the centre of the divot, or say 2 inches to the right of the ball.

Square the shaft to the target, and stand with your feet together and your hips and body central to the shaft.

Now move your left foot, say, 9 inches to the left of the shaft, and then your right foot EXACTLY the same distance to the right of the shaft for a drive; shorten the width for the shorter clubs.

Now bring the clubhead up to the ball with a one-piece movement of the right knee and hips to the left, and tilt the spine a little to the right so as to bring the head RIGHT OF CENTRE—THIS IS MOST IMPORTANT.

You must now check your distance from the ball and target line. Look at your hands. If, for a drive, they blot out your left toecap you are correct; if not, move away from the shot line until they do. For say an 8 iron, if they blot out your left ankle you are correct. The other clubs fall in between these two check points—that is somewhere in between the left toecap and the left ankle.

As so many golfers find it difficult to set up their stance by the Professionals' method, I recommend them to experiment with the mechanical method as it is more positive.

Make sure that your elbows are slightly shut to the shot line, as this ensures that your shoulders are in line with it, and the spine sufficiently tilted.

As most golfers have a kinky spine at its lower end, straighten it by contracting the abdominal muscles. This not only straightens the spine, but elevates the front of the pelvis basin and brings the hip joints forward and over the feet. This essential set is the BASIC FUNDAMENTAL, and is in fact the Masters' SECRET. I doubt if they are aware of this fact, but all of them possess it, for without it they could not possibly play as they do, for it is this set that enables them to move their hips in line with the plane of the swing and shoot them into the BOW. They derive their power and accuracy from their superb hip action. This set in the Masters' posture is, of course, the result of muscular development from an early age, but the late beginner can acquire it by the simple exercises which were described and illustrated in my first book, and are not beyond the ability of the average late beginner.

17. The Ladies at Impact

Of the ten action studies, the one I like the best is No. 1, Peggy Conley of the U.S.A. I consider it one that lady golfers anxious to improve their game could study with advantage.

Miss Conley may not have been so successful as a champion contender as some of the other players in this study, but this does not alter my view. Indeed, I would say that Miss Conley's action has the qualities of a champion.

It is a well-accepted fact that there are many champions who have highly individualistic actions. They have found the way that suits them to get the ball into the hole in the least number of strokes. It does not necessarily follow that they are good models for ordinary golfers to try and imitate. I am primarily concerned with the points that, in my view, will help handicap golfers.

These then are the points I consider worth noting about Miss Conley's action:

(*a*) She has BOTH ARMS fully extended immediately after impact, giving an excellent triangular formation of the arms and shoulder girdle. This indicates that she has used the big muscles of her legs and back to generate the motive power, and has used her arms to transmit the power to the clubhead.

(*b*) The action of her legs and hips—her pedestal—is well-nigh perfect.

Both legs are still bent, and the knees at the same level, and there has not been too much right heel lift at this point.

Her left hip has moved obliquely towards the left of the target, and given space for the right hip and shoulder to move laterally straight up the line of the shot.

Plate 15.
PEGGY CONLEY

(*c*) Note how her RIGHT HAND is 'brushing over' a RESISTING left hand, bringing the wrists almost at right angles to one another. This action has added LEVERAGE TO SWING, and keeps the clubface tight and square against the crushed ball until it reshapes itself.

This hand leverage is well worth mastering for it adds distance and accuracy to golf shots. Here is the drill for those who wish to add it to swing.

Let us assume that a stationary object like a door frame is a ball; place the clubface hard against it and adjust your stance as if at address; now bend the shaft into a bow to the left, using leftward pressure from your right knee and side, and at the same time turning or BRUSHING the right hand over your left hand, the latter resisting this pressure from the right hand by refusing to roll over, or the left arm from breaking at the elbow.

Now for its application when hitting balls. As the club is moving at quite a pace when approaching impact, this leverage has to be timed accurately, and as there is a time lag between mental stimulus of an action applied consciously and the muscular response, the effort to apply leverage has to take place some distance from impact. Trial and error is the only way the golfer can find out at what point in the down swing the effort has to be made, so that its effect will take place exactly at impact. If the effort feels like a PUSH ALONG, leverage has been applied too late. If it feels like a cross over of the wrists immediately after impact, it has been timed accurately.

It may be thought that such a leverage action will hook the ball. It may do so if applied too soon before impact, but if correctly timed it will not, because the concussion at impact between the club-face and the ball is so great—it can be anything between 5 cwt. and half a ton; the clubface does not turn until impact pressure is released, that is when the ball has gone.

(d) Note how Miss Conley's head is slightly behind the right knee—back and down—and that the clubhead is travelling LOW towards the target. This action is only possible when at address the head has been positioned RIGHT OF CENTRE. If, as is common practice with handicap golfers, it is positioned central to the feet or opposite the ball for the shorter shots, it is physically impossible to keep the head back and down without moving it to the right during the swing, which for the average golfer can be fatal. If I may be permitted to offer this young lady advice, I would suggest she positions her head a little more right of centre at address than she does at present and narrows her stance a fraction.

ANNE WELTS, of the U.S.A., a player of considerable achievements. I place her in the same category as Miss Conley.

She has similar qualities, and her after impact position is well worth studying.

There is just one point for comment. On the evidence of this photograph she may not be getting MAXIMUM power from her leg and body muscles. I say this because her right arm appears to be still slightly bent instead of being fully extended at this point.

Plate 16. ANNE WELTS.

ODILE GARAIALDE, of France. With one exception, I would place her in the same category as Miss Conley and Mrs. Welts.

My deduction from this photograph is that she has stood a little bit too close to the ball at address, and has had to rise on her toes to get the clubhead through. I would not recommend this action to handicap golfers, although great golfers like Bobby Jones and Joyce Wethered performed in this way.

Here are reliable checks for distance from the ball. For a drive, your hands should blot out your left toecap; for an 8 iron your left ankle; other clubs in between these two points—assuming, of course, that you have the 'K' address method of address established, and that your head is positioned RIGHT OF CENTRE.

Plate 17. ODILE GARAIALDE.   *Plate 18. PHYLLIS PREUSS.*

PHYLLIS PREUSS, of the U.S.A. This young lady has obviously developed a very useful left arm, but seems to have overlooked her right arm.

Her right arm is still bent a little after impact, so I would say that she has not made full use of her powerful-looking legs and her excellent hip action.

If a player wishes to gather up the power generated by the big muscles, it is necessary to have a fully EXTENDED triangle through impact.

The photograph seems to indicate that Miss Preuss has pulled the club down with the left arm from the top. I do not believe in this method for the average golfer who usually has a sloppy left arm. I consider it is much safer and produces better results if the upper arms are braced very firmly to the shoulder extremities, and make the whole assembly swing the clubhead. Most golfers operate better if they put their right side in control of the swing, particularly their

70

Plate 19. SHELLEY HAMLIN.   *Plate 20. CLAUDINE RUBIN.*

right shoulder, which if directed towards the right foot starting down seems to trigger off the down swing action in proper sequence, and with power.

Miss Preuss has her head nicely in position behind the right knee, which indicates that it was positioned right of centre at address, but the photograph also shows that her right hand is PUSHING the clubhead along instead of BRUSHING it over to add LEVERAGE to SWING.

SHELLEY HAMLIN, U.S.A. Both arms are not fully extended at this point, and because of this I think that power is being lost.

I have the impression that the address set-up has been too relaxed, particularly in regard to the upper arms, which I feel should be firmly braced to the shoulder extremities, and the set of the right leg from knee to foot, which I think should be set as a buttress in order to resist the back swing wind up pressures.

71

Plate 21. BRUGITTE VARANGOT *Plate 23.* ISA GOLDSCHMID

Plate 22. LOU DILL   *Plate 24.* ROBERTA ALBERS

I think that her right knee has kicked into the shot much too early, and has lost its valuable thrust during impact.

CLAUDINE RUBIN and BRUGITTE VARANGOT, of France. Both these young ladies appear to have kicked their right knee too early into the shot, and have therefore lost some power through impact. With this action, there is a danger of getting the hips so far ahead so that it is impossible to get the right hip and shoulder through correctly at impact, which can cause a quick hook.

LOU DILL, of the U.S.A. The impression I get from this photograph, is that there has been excessive hip action in relation to the rest of her body and legs. I dare say she has had to perform in this way to counter a HOOKER'S GRIP. Her left hand is in my view too much on top, and the right hand too much under the shaft. A golfer with this action is likely to develop spinal trouble, as the base of the spine has to accept a severe twist during impact at which point the greatest strain is on.

ISA GOLDSCHMID, of Italy, ROBERTA ALBERS, of the U.S.A. I think that both these young ladies have kicked their right knee too early into the shot, and used their right arm too late, and have therefore lost power generated by the big muscles. Too much swing, and not sufficient hit. One arm alone cannot possibly deliver the power to the blow, as can two when braced solidly to the shoulder extremities; nor can it control clubface alignment to the line of the shot as two can. Furthermore, hand leverage cannot be added to swing which puts the SNAP into the action of the Masters.

A golf club has an offset head—that is, it is angled to the shaft. It follows, therefore, that it requires two hands to control it. A cricket bat or tennis racquet have their handles fixed central to the striker so one hand can control them.

18. Casper's Smoothly Executed Swing

For quite a tallish man, Billy Casper has a rather narrow stance, so must have an exceptionally fine sense of balance.

His swing is one of the smoothest I have ever seen. There is not the slightest trace of violence in his action, yet his swing is by no means slow. It can be classified as the perfect One AND Two swing.

His set up at address is excellent. Strong corset and back muscles have straightened his lower spine and elevated the front of his pelvis basin—the hip joints are forward and over his feet, and not behind his heels. His head is erect, not lolling.

I regard Casper as a thoughtful, determined and very decisive golfer, who can concentrate well and quickly.

There is a solidness about his preparation and execution of the stroke. I would regard him as a FORWARD thinking golfer, with his mind working on the shot to the target rather more than on the ball.

Now let us see what can be learned from a study of these fine set of action photographs.

Plate 25. Casper stands solidly on RELAXED feet to the 'K' address.

His left arm and shaft are almost a straight radius, and his right arm is nicely angled to the club-shaft and in sympathy with the inward set of the right knee.

His head is positioned RIGHT OF CENTRE, the chin being level with the inner edge of the right knee.

His weight pressure seems slightly more on the right foot than on the left–about 60/40.

I would say that he is kneeling rather than sitting at address so as

Plate 25.   Plate 26.   Plate 27.

Plate 28.   Plate 29.   Plate 30.

to bring his centre of gravity more over his feet.

In gripping the clubshaft, he has drawn his right hand hard up against the left index finger, crushing it as it were, against the other three fingers.

75

Plate 31. Plate 32. Plate 33.

Plate 34. Plate 35. Plate 36.

N.B. This small point is very important, for the squeeze FIRMS the left hand finger grip, without having to contract the finger muscles excessively.

Note his shoes, they have LOW HEELS. Standard height of shoes in

Plate 37.   Plate 38.   Plate 39.

Plate 40.   Plate 41.   Plate 42.

general are too high for golf, and tend to push the golfer on to the soles of his feet during impact.

Plates 26–34. Practically all the swinging movement in this segment of the back swing is taking place as the result of a rightward

Plate 43.   Plate 44.   Plate 45.

Plate 46.   Plate 47.   Plate 48.

turning action of the torso from the shoulder extremities to the waist.

The inclination of the spine ensures that the shoulder extremities move in a fairly steep spiral sweep relative to the plane of the swing.

78

Plate 49.　　　　　Plate 50.　　　　　Plate 51.

Plate 52.　　　　　Plate 53.　　　　　Plate 54.

Keeping the clubface square to the plane of the swing influences the shoulder sweep.

The pedestal—from feet to hip joints, is resisting the torso wind up—somewhat like a shock absorber on a car upon the action of the road springs. Obviously there is some yield in the pedestal muscles, but NONE IN THE RIGHT KNEE; this is very important. The right leg from the knee to the foot, the RIGHT SHIN POST, must hold fast against the wind up pressures, for with the left knee drag it triggers off the down swing with leftward thrust.

The shoulders and arms, in the form of a triangle, firmly braced at the shoulder extremities, move in ONE PIECE to take the clubhead back from the moment of take off; there must be no alteration in this triangular assembly for the first half of the back swing, and very little subsequently. In the execution of the 'one piece' take off, the motive power feels as if it comes from the shoulder extremities—that is the base of the triangle.

An important point in Casper's backswing action, is the way he keeps the clubface at right angles to the plane of the swing. This is not a natural action, and to some extent is difficult to master, but it has to be mastered if you want to play well.

It can be acquired by practice, swinging a club with a determination of reaching the top of the swing with the RIGHT WRIST AND HAND UNDER THE SHAFT; there is no need to hurry to reach the top. Just get the right image you want at the top, and leave it to your brain to provide the action—it will. There are two important reasons for this action. One is that it prevents the left wrist from buckling IN and UNDER the shaft and opening the clubface—a very common and disastrous fault; the other is that it WINDS UP THE RIGHT FOREARM MUSCLES which puts them in the position to add LEVERAGE to SWING as the clubhead meets the ball at impact. The old Masters used to refer to this 'twisting action' as 'WRINGING THE FLANNEL'—quite a good discription.

Plates 35–40. This is a point in the swing at which the muscular wind up of the great back muscles tends to lift the left heel too high from the ground, or force the hip joints to turn too much and collapse, especially with those golfers who are a bit corpulent or who have kinky spines. In such cases the solution is to kneel a bit more and firm up the abdominal muscles at address.

You will notice that Casper's hips have yielded very little in relation to the turn of the shoulders and his left heel is still near the ground.

Contrary to common belief, the hands are made to reverse the clubhead at the top with an IN to OUT LOOP, and not as one might imagine an OUT to IN loop. This action is the result of a leftward thrust from the right foot and a leftwards drag from the left leg, accompanied by a reverse turn of the hips as they move to the left, but because of the considerable turn of the shoulders by the masters during the back swing there is sufficient margin left to enable the hands to move outwards and still move through impact STRAIGHT UP THE LINE of the shot, and not across it from OUT to IN. Where handicap golfers go wrong in this top segment is that, when reaching the top, they get the impression that in order to come back to the ball from IN to OUT they must prepare for this by trying to bring their HANDS from OUT to IN as they reverse the swing. At this point the hands must remain passive and obey the knee and hip action. If you compare the hand position of Casper at waist level going back, with the hand position at the same level coming down, you will see that the hands are much further from the waist coming down, but the clubhead is at this point much closer in, and acutely angled to the left arm. This profoundly important action is the result of keeping the wrists, especially the right wrist, very relaxed as the club is halted and reversed, by the motive power coming from the big muscles of the legs and back. The arms must be DRAGGED DOWN, not PUSHED down.

Plates 41 and 42. At this point in the swing, you will note that the shaft lies along the ROOTS of the fingers of the left hand, with the left thumb well down the shaft, its tip actually under the right thumb. The shaft, which at address was placed obliquely across the left hand, has therefore moved to the roots of the fingers; if it were not for this change of alignment as the club is put into reverse, it would be physically impossible for these great players, and others for that matter, to acutely angle the club to the left arm, the late hitting angle or what I call the COMET's TAIL.

This essential change of clubshaft alignment to the left hand calls for a grip that is firm but not tight. It can be found by trial and error according to the strength of one's fingers. Thickness of the grip and the length of one's fingers have a profound influence on this essential.

I suggest you make this test. Swing with both hands to the top, having started with the shaft placed obliquely across the left palm and closed the fingers tightly round the shaft. Then at the top, stop, and have a look at the left hand grip, and gradually relax the finger grip until the shaft drops into alignment with the roots of the fingers; note the strength of the grip that enables the readjustment to happen, and adopt this at address.

If your grips are shiny or worn, whether leather or rubber, ask your Professional to replace them AT ONCE to a thickness that suits you; nothing ruins golf action more than defective grips. If you have dry hands, my advice is use good quality rubber grips, and before playing a round hold your hands in hot water for a few moments. Rubber grips should be washed fairly often with toilet soap and water. If you prefer leather grips, my advice is to ask your Professional to keep them in good order for you. Leather will perish or dry out if neglected, and become slippery, without being aware of it, you will tighten your hold on the club excessively and ruin your game

Plates 43–45. Note how the weight is being transferred OBLIQUELY from the sole of the right foot onto the heel of the left foot, activated by a thrust from the right foot and leftward drag from the left knee. Coupled with this leftward thrust, the left hip turns away from the shot line leaving sufficient room for the right knee, hip and shoulder to come STRAIGHT UP THE LINE and deliver a straight line blow through the ball. A blow delivered in a straight line applies more extended power than one delivered in a curve.

Plates 46–48. Casper's knees and legs have not straightened because he uses them to put a FLAT in the arc of the swing during impact. They shuttle along with both knees in the same plane. Robert Jones of America referred to this segment action as FREE WHEELING through impact.

Note that the triangular formation of the shoulders and arms is still intact. This is clear evidence that these great golfers use the big strong muscles of their legs and back to provide the motive power, which in turn is filtered through their SHOULDER EXTREMITIES, especially the RIGHT one. Their arms convey this motive power to the club, they do not produce it as so many handicap golfers try to do. When it is realised that the pull of the club upon the golfer can vary from zero to as much as 60 lb., it must be obvious that human arm muscles have not sufficient strength to GO IT ALONE. To say that golf is all hands is in my view wrong if the expression means MUSCULAR ACTION; on the other hand, if it means they are the 'switchboard', I will agree that this is true, particularly with the COMPLETE GOLFER whose co-ordinated actions are BUILT IN. There is no doubt that the hands transmit clubhead movement to the brain and the brain sends the appropriate messages back to muscles that will produce the action—not necessarily the right action. This will depend on the knowledge and experience of the golfer, enabling him to set up images of the action he desires.

You will note that Casper's head has stayed back of centre and is now slightly behind the advanced position of the right knee. In remaining back of centre the heavy head is acting as a counter-weight to the hips as they move into the BOW. His eyes are still looking at the spot on which the ball rested at address.

Plates 49–54.

19. How to Improve Your Short Game

Almost every club golfer can greatly improve their short game if they will follow the drill described in this chapter.

First let me say that most golfers fail to equal the Masters because of bad stance alignment, bad posture, and incorrect head placement. All three can be put right quite simply when you know how.

Take, say, a 6 or 7 iron, with a dozen balls, on to the practice ground and set them up in line about 6 inches apart so that you have not to stoop too often.

Place the clubhead on the ground behind the ball, and lay your hands opposite a point which would be the centre of the divot you should take with this iron—that is the bottom of the swing.

With the hands held still in this position, move your feet into position, so that a line through your elbows indicates that they are slightly shut to the target line—this ensures that your shoulders are not open but square to the shot.

Check your grip to see that one knuckle of the left hand and two knuckles of the right hand are visible.

Check the placement of your head to see that your nose is immediately above the inside of your right knee when it is braced in slightly towards centre, and set firmly so that it will not move during the back swing. If all is correct, you should be looking obliquely at the back of the ball.

Now adjust your distance from the ball and target line. If you are correct, and are using, say, a 7 iron, your hands should blot out your left ankle, from your vision. You are now ready to take off.

Have a few waggles to reduce tension, and before regrounding the clubhead behind the ball CONTRACT THE ABDOMINAL MUSCLES until you feel a firming up of your buttocks—your seat. Brace the upper arms firmly to your shoulder extremities, and take off with an immediate backward hinging of your right wrist, which to you may feel that you are hooding or shutting the clubface—this is as it should be.

Plate 55.   Plate 56.   Plate 57.

Plates 55, 56 and 57. Syd Scott. Even in a delicate shot like the short pitch the BIG MUSCLES should still be in control. The left wrist has been kept in line with the left forearm and the right wrist has hinged square to the plane of the swing—the clubface is cuddled. The execution of this stroke is excellent in all departments. The rocking shoulders—the base of the triangle—have provided the propelling power.

20. What I Think of Bobby Cole

It is my considered opinion that this bright young man has a successful future in front of him. He has got most of the stuff champions are made of.

The photographs in this chapter are well worth studying.

Plates 58 and 59 were taken while we were discussing the importance of possessing a wide yielding thumb for golf.

I would like you to note in plate 58, how a continuation of the upper spine cuts through the ear, a relationship that should be maintained in the address position. With a great many club players, a continuation of the spinal line passes the back of their heads—'the Lolling Head'. Note also from the same photo how the shaft lies along the roots of his fingers, with the thumb fully extended, yet well angled back to the wrist.

Plate 60. Here you have an almost perfect golf POSTURE. It may not be elegant, but it is No. 1. Basic Fundamental. With such a posture, almost every other action movement is simple to apply without conscious thought. The Villain in golf is the figure S posture; the correct posture is the Masters' secret, and I doubt whether they are aware of this fact for they have never had to experience personally the effect that BOTH have on golf action. Most, if not all of the Masters' started on the journey to stardom before their postures were destroyed by SOFT LIVING, but even they can fall apart if they neglect to keep their corset and spinal muscles in trim.

Note how Cole's pelvis basin is forward and high in front, and how straight his spine is from the shoulder blades to his tail—no protruding buttocks here.

Plate 58.

Plate 59.

Plate 60.

This body set is common to almost all great golfers and enables them to move their hip mass correctly along the line of the shot and into the BOW. There is no scything action in their hip action to ruin what should take place above their pedestal.

Very few adult beginners possess a good posture for golf, but by quite simple exercises I have already described and illustrated in my first book a correct posture can be established within a few months and can enable most golfers to reach single figures or even scratch.

The alternative to exercises is disappointing and tiring golf, lost tempers, and quite likely spinal damage such as disc trouble.

Plate 61. Here you see what I have often referred to as the proud 'K' address posture.

The head is held up, and the chin in, no LOLLING.

The arms are EXTENDED, and the upper arms are nicely braced into the chest to ensure that the shoulder extremities can take charge of the one piece take away; by one piece is meant that the shoulders as the base of the triangle formed by them and the arms, start the propulsion as a one piece assembly.

The wrists are held up; it is a mistake to break them downwards, which is a common failing with most golfers.

The knees are bent, and the right knee is nicely set in to resist the back swing pressures like a SHIN POST stuck in the ground.

The feature of the 'K' address is that the clubshaft and left arm are almost in a straight line, and the eye-line to the BACK of the ball passes about 2 inches to the right of the hands, and the head is positioned RIGHT OF CENTRE, where it will remain until after impact. The majority of club golfers position their head CENTRAL TO THEIR FEET, and then wonder why they lift their head. The club is not attached to one's nose; the centre of the swing from address to impact is the left shoulder extremity, and this extremity MUST be positioned exactly opposite the BOTTOM OF THE SWING, so it follows that the players head must be at least 6 inches to the right of this point.

Plate 61.   *Plate 62.*

Plate 62. Top of the swing.

The wrists and elbows are close together.

The right forearm muscles have been wound up by bringing the right wrist and hand UNDER the shaft, and this in turn prevents the left wrist from being forced in and under the shaft. It has also moved the clubshaft into the ROOTS of the fingers of the left hand, and thereby established the ACUTE ANGLE—the Comet's Tail—between the left arm and the shaft.

The right hand and wrist in this very desirable position makes them act like a platform, and take the weight of the club—which could be as much as 12 lb. The left hand being further away from

89

Plate 63.

Plate 64.

Plate 65.

the clubhead than the right hand, the left arm is PULLED STRAIGHT, not pushed straight.

Note how the right shin post and left toe peg have held fast against the wind up pressures. Considerable muscular strain is felt up the inside of the shins at this point. The left leg is now ready to DRAG the hips towards the target, and the right to assist the action by THRUST in the same direction.

Plate 63. The Down Swing.

Note how the LEFT KNEE is applying leftward DRAG upon the hips, and the right knee is about to shoot the weight up the line. This leg action seen in this excellent photo actually takes place a fraction before the backward momentum of the swing has been halted and reversed; its feel is like a leftward TWISTING ACTION of the knees. It is difficult to cultivate, but well worth mastering.

When the knees have reached this position, I am of the opinion that the next move is to drive the RIGHT SHOULDER STRAIGHT DOWN TOWARDS THE RIGHT FOOT, dragging the arms, hands and club along with it. To try and bring the club down with the hands and arms independently is definitely wrong, their job at this point is to remain firm but passive attachments to the shoulder extremities. The gap between the hands and the right shoulder extremity MUST be LOCKED and not allowed any freedom until the hands have reached waist level.

Those of my readers who wish to master this splendid and effective action should perform the following drill.

Go to the top as in *Plate 62* and lock the hands to the right shoulder as if with a strap. Now bring the hips over and round with DRAG from the left knee, and thrust leftward from the right knee, as you will have no clubhead momentum, inertia, to retard your shoulders from turning, try and hold them still. The left knee drag may give you the sensation that you are squatting slightly with the hips. At this point drive the right shoulder, hands and arms assembly straight down towards the right foot.

Having accomplished this drill, start from the address and complete the full swing in the sequence described; keep moving, but apply the greatest effort in arriving at *Plate 63* position before you have completed the back swing, and don't hurry the action. Give yourself time to complete the SHUNT.

Plate 64. IMPACT. A very revealing action photo.

The substantial thrust from the right foot has now cleared the left hip out of the way and given free passage for the right hip, shoulder and arm to move straight towards the target.

Centrifugal force and gravity have pulled the shaft of the club straight to the left arm.

The hands have ADDED LEVERAGE TO SWING which keeps the clubhead hard against the distorted ball until it reshapes itself. Immediately this concussion pressure between ball and clubface is released, the right hand will BRUSH OVER the left hand which is trying to take place during impact. Photos do not show this leverage at the time it is being applied because impact pressures cancel it out. This obscure hand leverage is well worth cultivating, and the best way to master it is to place a clubhead against a door frame as though addressing a ball, and bend the shaft by the leverage described; this trains the muscles to apply it on the ball.

Note the position of the head in relation to the right foot and right knee—it is behind centre, or a fraction more than it was positioned at address. It would certainly not have held back in opposition to the hips moving forward, unless at address it had been positioned right of centre, with the eyes focussed on the backside of the ball, giving it, as it were an OBLIQUE look. Golfers must train themselves to master these unnatural alignments, even for the tiddlers round the green—putting excepted.

Judging from the photograph, I would say that it shows up a weak spot in the left arm. I think it should be fully extended at this point to ensure accuracy in direction.

Plate 65.

I asked Bobby Cole to swing a club to the top with his left arm only. At the first attempt his left arm crumpled up. The photo shows the second attempt which was executed at half the speed of the first.

This satisfied me that it was his right hand, wrist and arm that supported the club at the top of the swing as a platform, and that the left arm acted as a BEAM.

You will see that his left thumb is not under the shaft but more at the side of it. In such a position it cannot support the leverage from the club, so his left wrist and fingers have had to accept the strain. This would be physically impossible in an all-out swing, which could raise the cantileverage of the club from 7 to about 12 lb.

Golfers who endeavour to swing the club mainly with the left arm should remember this and switch the control to the right hand and arm, making sure that their intention is to have the right hand and wrist UNDER the shaft at the top.

21. Playing with Sway may be Your Way

There are many club golfers who find it difficult, even alarming in some cases, to POSITION THEIR HEAD RIGHT OF CENTRAL, and keep it there throughout the swing.

For some reason there is an unconscious urge to bring the eyes opposite the ball about to be struck, so they shift the head back to centre as they come in for impact.

It follows, therefore, that if the head shifts to the left so will the shoulders, so at impact the left shoulder—the centre of the swing—is much too far ahead, and the shot is ruined.

For those who find it difficult to keep their head back and down at impact, here is a method which can be most effective, although it is unorthodox.

When addressing the ball, position the head central to the feet. At the start of the back swing allow the head to follow the swing for 4 or 5 inches, no more, and keep it there for the remainder of the swing, but see that the sway is done very slowly.

You will of course feel SWAY to the right, that is as it should be, but be careful to see that the right leg from the knee to the foot—the RIGHT SHIN POST—does not yield or the leg straighten, for it is the thrust from this knee and foot that triggers off the down swing by sending the knees towards the target, turns the hips, rocks the shoulders, and DRAGS the hands, arms and club down from the top, and in that order.

Golfers who have put on weight round the hips and abdomen, and therefore find it difficult to make a full pivot, will find this

'TOP SWAY' method very helpful. It seems to produce a smooth flowing action from the right hip, and a feeling that the HANDS ARE COMING UP THE LINE FROM BEHIND THE HEELS.

PLAY WITH SWAY MIGHT PROVE TO BE YOUR WAY, so why not have a go, but see you do it SLOWLY.

There is another way to execute sway by what could be called the STEPPING OFF method—here it is for you to test.

Take up a stance about 5 inches narrower than usual, say the length of your shoe or narrower. Then to start the swing, step off 4 or 5 inches to the right with your right foot, allowing your weight and head to come on to this foot and then keep your head still until after impact.

Provided you execute the shift slowly and deliberately, it is possible to add considerable length to your shots. For some reason this method keeps the weight behind the blow and makes it flow into the shot at and after impact.

CENTRE

THE SOLID LINES indicate the first position, and how the HEAD is CENTRAL to the feet at address. THE BROKEN LINES show the second position and how the HEAD and SHOULDERS have moved to the RIGHT OF CENTRE at the start of the swing. The RIGHT KNEE, however, has not moved from its first position.

The head is then KEPT STILL in its second position throughout the remainder of the swing, so that at IMPACT it will be BEHIND the CENTRAL LINE, and therefore behind the ball.

Fig. 7.

95

22. The Secret of the Masters' Loop

I have often wondered why this profoundly important feature in a really good golf swing is overlooked.

Doubtless, with the Masters, it is BUILT IN to their action, and therefore unrecognised, but so far as the club golfer is concerned, I believe its absence is caused because they are so often reminded that they must endeavour to bring the clubhead into the ball from IN to OUT, so it is natural that they should start the action as they commence the down swing, so they try and bring their hands INWARDS as they reverse the club.

Unfortunately, this effort has the effect of preventing the hips and legs from LEADING the down swing. When this happens the arms and hands take charge, and undo their inward loop by sending the clubhead away from their axis, and finally into the ball from OUT to IN.

In a well-executed swing, the hips and knees actually start moving to the left BEFORE the backward motion of the hands and club have been halted and reversed. Unless this is achieved, it is impossible for the right shoulder to DESCEND before it comes round. Let us see why this happens.

The shoulders and spine are like the letter 'T' with the hip mass attached to its tail like a pendulum weight, so it follows that the hip mass must carry the bottom of the spine over to the left in order to ROCK the shoulders before they can turn.

Here is a simple drill that will educate the muscles of your legs to produce this important LOOPING action.

Swing the club smoothly to the top—over yourself and not round

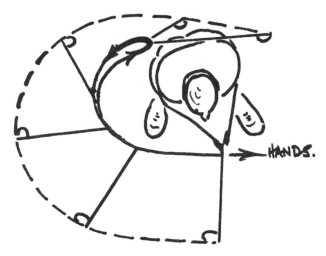

HANDS.

Fig. 8. Bird's eye view of the 'IN to OUT' Hand Loop as the swing is reversed.

This essential loop is caused by the hips turning and sliding laterally leftwards, slightly in advance of the start of the down swing. To loop from OUT to IN is wrong and indicates that the hip shift has been delayed, and the arms have taken charge.

Fig. 9. Right side view of the Hand Loop. Correct. The hips have turned and shifted leftwards, slightly in advance of the start of the down swing. This hip action has pushed the hand outwards and brings them down. Impact will be slightly from IN to OUT.

Incorrect. The hips are late in turning and sliding leftwards. Hands and arms have taken charge and looped inwards. Impact will be from OUT to IN.

This may be contrary to common-sense, but it is the correct advance action of the hips that governs the swing arc.

yourself—with both legs nicely flexed at the knees, and STOP.

When at the top, with a leftward push from the RIGHT KNEE and a leftward DRAG from the LEFT KNEE, shift the hips about 6 inches to the left and STOP.

Make this movement DRAG the arms, hands and RIGHT SHOULDER downwards in ONE SOLID PIECE. On no account allow the arms to break the triangle assembly—they must remain inert.

Having mastered this exercise, start again, but this time endeavour to perform the 'KNEE SHUTTLE' action a fraction in advance of the arms and hands completing the back swing.

This is easier said than done, but it can be mastered with perseverance, providing it is not rushed.

The feeling generated by this ADVANCED knee and hip action is as follows:

1. The shift feels as if the hips and knees are exerting a leftward twisting action.

2. You should feel that the hands have moved slightly towards the ball and target line—this is the loop.

3. You should feel that when the shift is in progress your hip mass has descended slightly, a kind of SQUATTING action activated by an increased yield at the knees.

4. You should feel that the left shoulder has ascended without turning.

When you next watch the Masters in action, note how their hips and knees start moving to the left before they reverse the swing. You will see this best when facing them front or back.

Then stand to their right hand side, and watch for the IN to OUT loop performed by their hands as a result of their hip and knee action—a twisting action. You will see this best if you focus your eyes at the point where their hands will reach at the top of the swing, adjacent to their right shoulder extremity. Watch the Master when he is practising: there is more space around him, and he may be willing to show you the action in slow motion.

23. Letters from Readers

MR. X SO HELPFUL

I have been a regular reader of *Golf Monthly* for some five years now and consider it far and away the best periodical in the world.

The articles by Mr. X are of a particularly refreshing nature, and I'm sure they helped me to bring my handicap down to four.

I. J. M. Morrison,
Kingston 8,
Jamaica

BALANCING OF PUTTERS

I have made copies of the articles by Mr. X which appeared in *Golf Monthly* about the balancing of putters, and have shown them to several Professionals and national Amateur champions in this country.

All of them tell me it has markedly improved their putting. It gives them a different feel of the putter and aids not only in hitting the ball more squarely, but aids in the follow through of the putter as well. . . .

Professor John C. Ullery,
Columbus, Ohio, U.S.A.

RIGHT SHOULDER ACTION

Mr. X's article in the April issue on the action of the shoulder is right in every respect, and will be helpful to a great many people. Tommy Jacobs and Gardner Dickinson play and teach this right shoulder action as demonstrated by Mr. X. I think this particular phase of the swing could be further developed.

Emmet McCarthy,
Chicago,
U.S.A.

POSITIVE ATTACK

I have been a regular reader of your contributions to *Golf Monthly* and I would say that the article which has helped me most has been your study on POSTURE, the 'K' style.

I have tried out your present method, the 'Gap Lock', and find it has given me a new conception of the required down swing action. By this I mean no conscious effort is needed.

I visualise a positive attack with the right shoulder movement, bringing the shoulder and elbow close in to the right side, which drives the hips and knees leftward into what you describe as the bowed position at impact, not overlooking the firm left wrist working 'convex' not 'concave'.

In other words, the method you outline sparks off a series of chain reactions.

This gives me a positive action to work on, and I thank you very much.

David Lewis,
Penarth, GLAM.

LOCKING THE GAP

I was delighted to read your article about 'Locking the Gap' in the April issue. It describes the down swing technique which I hit upon by different reasoning two years ago, and which improved my rather poor game considerably.

I have noticed how few golf writers explain how to achieve the desirable pre-impact position with the right elbow cranked into the side shortly before contact with the ball.

I suffered from letting the wrists go at the top and consequently lost much clubhead speed at impact. I reasoned that, physically, it was impossible to keep the wrists cocked down to waist level, unless the right elbow remained cranked, and that the right elbow could not remain cranked unless the right shoulder came down first.

In concentrating upon the downward movement of the right shoulder first in the down swing, I found an immediate improvement in striking the ball, and in the length and direction achieved.

It took me many years of indifferent golf, and much reading of books and wrong practising, before, at 51 years, I managed to find a basis for a reasonable game.

I thought you might be interested in these comments, since your article has a similar thesis. I would think that many of those who follow your advice will improve their game.

John L. Williams,
Thames Ditton

HANDICAP DOWN 12

Having come down the handicap scale from 20 to 8 in 18 months, I take all tips, read and oral, very seriously and try them all, remembering only those which improve my game.

This brings me to the point of thanking you for your Mr. X article in the November issue 'How to pitch and putt better'.

I looked back at a recent cine film taken of me while playing, and the diagram on your page was myself—the one with the sagging back.

After practising, holding my pelvis in, I find it makes me a better striker of the ball. I now wish to strengthen myself in this weakness.

T. Hardy, Immingham

PROFESSIONAL PRAISES MR. X

I am a golf instructor at a 9-hole par-3 course and driving range in Torrance, California, and a good friend and subscriber of your magazine, Roy E. Priebe, has given me various copies to read, and I wish to advise that I enjoy the magazine very much.

I read and study golf constantly trying to improve the art of teaching how to swing a golf club, and I have found your magazine very helpful.

I wish to comment on one of your writers in particular for his simple and very understanding articles and drawings, and that would have to be Mr. X. My regards to the very fine gentleman.

John Arnold,
Torrance, California

A TWO HANDICAP GOLFER THANKS MR. X

Through your columns may I send greetings to all my old golfing friends in Ireland.

They might be interested to know that, chiefly due to your Mr. X, I am still playing to a 2 handicap, although I'll be a senior golfer next birthday. Go to it lads!

Bill McCormick,
Queensland, AUSTRALIA

Golf Monthly's Lessons with Mr. X

For those readers who have not had an opportunity to read the author's first book here are the chapters in it. Copies are still available.

1. The Importance of Posture
2. The Grip
3. Stance and Address—the 'K' Set-up
4. The Human Pedestal
5. Balance and Weight Movement
6. The Swing
7. The Duty of the Hands—Adding Leverage to Swing
8. Control and Timing
9. The Short Game—On and Around the Greens
10. Home Exercises
11. Your Golf Equipment
12. Analysis of Master Golfers: Jack Nicklaus and Ken Venturi
    Letters from Readers of the Mr. X Articles to *Golf Monthly*